Kayaking with Eric Jackson

Whitewater Paddling
Strokes & Concepts

Eric Jackson

Photos by Skip Brown

Sanctioned by the
World Kayak Federation

STACKPOLE
BOOKS

Published by
STACKPOLE BOOKS
5067 Ritter Road
Mechanicsburg PA 17055
www:stackpolebooks.com

Printed in China

FIRST EDITION

10 9 8 7 6 5 4 3 2

Cover photos by Skip Brown

Library of Congress Cataloging-in-Publication Data
Jackson, Eric, 1964-
     Whitewater paddling: strokes & concepts/Eric Jackson:
photos by Skip Brown.—1st ed.
       p.   cm. (Kayaking with Eric Jackson)
    ISBN 0-8117-2997-4
     1. Whitewater canoeing. 2. Kayaking. I Title. II Series: Jackson, Eric, 1964-
Kayaking with Eric Jackson.
GV788.J32 1999 99-17547
797.1'224—dc21
                                         CIP

Contents

Preface ix

Getting Started with the Twelve-Minute Stroke Drill Warm-up xi

1. Basic Strokes and Concepts 1

    Forward Stroke 3

    Reverse Stroke 7

    Primary Turning Strokes 11

        Forward Sweep 12

        Reverse Sweep 16

    Secondary Turning Strokes 19

        Draws 20

        C-Stroke 25

        S-Turn Stroke 28

        Offside C-Stroke 33

        Reverse Compound Stroke 37

        Sideslip Stroke 41

        Reverse Sweep Torso Drill 44

        Squirts 46

        Initiation Stroke (Playboating) 52

2. Applying the Strokes and Concepts to Whitewater 55

    Four Whitewater Concepts 55

    Eddy Turns 57

        Peel Out 57

        Eddy Out 60

    Ferrying 64

    Whitewater S-Turns 67

    Holes 71

    Wave Surfing 77

Thanks to Sean Long and Danny Stock for teaching me how to write. This was my first crack at writing a book, and since engineering was my chosen major, I needed lots of help. Sean, a professional editor, spent countless hours making my manuscript presentable. Danny, a member of the U.S. Junior Slalom Team, and the person best trained in the EJ Strokes and Concepts program, spent just as much time making sure that my message wasn't lost when transferred to paper. Thanks to you both for your efforts.

Skip Brown, one of the world's best whitewater photographers, made this book much more attractive and effective through his skill, effort, and many, many rolls of film.

All of my coaches and fellow athletes made possible the knowledge I now possess.

Scott Shipley taught me how to think for myself in developing new skills and techniques.

My wife Kristine made my life of paddling possible and nothing would happen without that freedom.

Preface

I expect to be living the rest of my life in the future. I want to be relatively sure what kind of future that is going to be. That is my reason for planning.

—Paxton Hood

At the same time I was putting together an instructional program for the World Kayak Federation, I spent two years developing and improving a strokes and concepts course that I taught in Washington DC. The most difficult part of refining this course was replacing, 'old school' practice techniques with 'new school' ones; I was an old school boater for a long time before I became a new school boater, and those old habits die hard.

I'm proud to present this book, the first to approach kayaking from a new school style of instruction. This book brings the fundamentals of whitewater paddling to you that will take you from where you are in your paddling skills to where you want to be. The beauty of kayaking is found in the basics of paddling, and a proper understanding and execution of the basics is the best way to establish a solid foundation to plan for your future in the sport.

See you on the river!

Getting Started with the 12-Minute Stroke Drill Warm-up

This book introduces strokes and concepts that are part of a bigger picture. Each one is simple in its pure form, which makes it easy to learn. Once you can perform the strokes in their pure form, you will have the rest of your paddling career to become a master of them in whitewater. Each stroke's technique has to be near perfect and become a habit in flatwater before you use it in whitewater. Only after you learn the strokes and understand the concepts in flatwater can you practice them and make them automatic. The 12-minute stroke drill warm-up will make that process as short as possible.

First read the descriptions of the strokes and try to visualize them. Then take the list to a river or lake with you and try to do them. Most will come easily, and if you are a skilled kayaker, you will be able to perform them almost immediately; others will come with difficulty. Initially you won't be able to do the warm-up drills in twelve minutes, but once you've learned to do all of the drills and have the routine memorized, you will be able to complete all of the drills in flatwater in twelve minutes.

Your goal is to learn the stroke drills by heart in flatwater, and then do them each time you paddle. You can practice them in flatwater, in an eddy, or in easy whitewater. Once you are at this stage, you should be perfecting the drills in flatwater and beginning to apply the drills to whitewater. There are a number of key drills that teach you how to use the energy of the water to turn your paddle into a keel and a sail, thus capturing the river's energy and getting you from point A to point B with more speed and less energy. At this point you will begin to automatically use your new skills in whitewater, and your new techniques will overcome your old habits. You will also be able to coach yourself and others, because you will have a working understanding of what is possible on the water. By using your drills in whitewater, you will be able to monitor your progress. You will no longer have to guess what your weaknesses are.

Mixed in with each stroke are the fundamental rules of boat control, which will help you put the whole package together. Each section ends with a list of highlights so that you can use this book as a quick reference guide. Three levels of awareness are listed for each stroke so that you can continue to improve your skills no matter what level you have achieved.

Let's get to it!

Basic Strokes and Concepts

Before learning the specific strokes, concepts, and drills, there are a few general guidelines you need to make habits of as you work on learning new strokes and refining your techniques.

MAINTAIN GOOD POSTURE

There are three postures you can have in a kayak: forward, in which you are leaning forward at the waist and putting weight on your heels; neutral, in which you are putting all of the weight on your butt; and back, in which you are leaning back and holding yourself up with your knees.

PADDLE IN THE FORWARD POSITION

- This keeps you on the offensive. Your brain has two orientations when you are kayaking: offensive and defensive. See your body as a light switch. Forward is on, backward is off. It's that simple. Pay attention to your paddling and see what you do when you get scared, indecisive, or surprised. Chances are that you lean back. When you lean forward, you are much more apt to act instead of react. Be on the offensive; paddle in the forward position. (Fig. 1)
- This keeps you in control. Staying forward keeps your bow down and your stern edges out of the water. Most flips are caused by the stern catching an edge.
- This keeps you in position for your strokes. Most of your strokes require a forward or neutral position.

FIG. 1 Proper forward posture.

USE A GOOD GRIP

Hold your paddle on your head. Your elbows should form right angles. This is the 90-degree rule. This position, the same used when bench-pressing or doing chin-ups, is the strongest for pulling and pushing. If you use right-hand control, your left wrist should remain straight during the push to avoid cocking the wrist down and losing power.

ALWAYS LEAVE A MARGIN FOR ERROR

Always leave a margin for error when paddling. Taking this approach may save your life. Short of that, you will be more likely to make your lines when running rivers, have clean runs on a slalom course, and stay in holes during rodeos, and you'll have a greater percentage of successful attempts while kayaking, which will increase your confidence.

Leaving a margin for error doesn't mean that you have to paddle conservatively. It means being aware of what you're trying to accomplish when approaching rapids and ensuring that you'll succeed even if you make a mistake. And it means practicing all of your moves in a river so that even if you roll, lose your angle, or miss an eddy, you'll know what to do. Margin for error applies in every aspect of

paddling, from your equipment to your roll. If you drop your paddle, can you hand roll? Some practice learning hand rolling gives you a big margin for that error.

It takes practice to see lines that give you margin for error. For example, if you have a big, important ferry to make a big drop, you should look to see if you can attain up an eddy before you start the ferry in case you miss the ferry. You should always know in advance what eddy you will catch next. You also need to know what the aggressive line is so that you know the difference. Practice taking shorter lines and leaving no margin for error in safe rapids to see how consistent you are in making the ferries, eddies, and moves. This teaches you how much margin for error you really need in order to be 100 percent sure about every move. Remember that your skill level varies based on how much you have been paddling recently and the familiarity you have with the river and your equipment.

Ultimately, mistakes happen to everybody. The more consideration you give to having a margin for error in every aspect of your paddling, the less your mistakes will affect you or others.

Bearing the above in mind, let's look at the specific strokes.

STROKE	Forward Stroke
DRILL	Take 200 forward strokes: 100 slow, 50 medium, 50 fast
GOALS	To take your current physical abilities and maximize the power, speed, and control you have in your kayak

Focus on the techniques below during these two hundred strokes and, ultimately, on every forward stroke you take. A good forward stroke improves your ability to make difficult moves such as attainments, ferries, boofs, and eddy turns, and is critical for rodeo and slalom racing as well. A good whitewater forward stroke has three important elements: proper paddle position and movement, proper body position and movement, and proper boat position and movement.

PADDLE POSITION AND MOVEMENT

The paddle blade goes in the water at the toes and comes out at the hip

- This is pulling the boat from the bow, which is a much more effective way to move the boat than pushing from the middle or stern. (Fig. 2–3)
- This keeps the boat under control in whitewater. Pulling the boat eliminates excess yaw (movement left to right).
- You are ready for the next stroke, whether it be a forward or control stroke.

The paddle is nearly vertical

- This maximizes efficiency and control. A vertical paddle is the most effective, as it pulls the boat straight forward without causing it to yaw. A boat that doesn't yaw goes faster and is easier to keep under control.

The top hand stays near the helmet at eye level, and the arm is never fully extended

- Most people focus on pushing the top hand out front forcefully, but this causes the paddle blade angle to lift water at the end. Pushing the top hand often causes you to pull on the paddle blade before it is fully planted in the water.

BODY POSITION AND MOVEMENT

Your body is like a spring that you can wind up and unwind. The forward stroke is most powerful when you initially wind up the torso, then plant the paddle in the water, then unwind. (Fig. 4–6) To understand the importance of torso rotation, try this exercise: Sit on the floor with your legs extended, your back straight, and your shoulders back. Keeping your shoulder line fixed, extend your right arm straight out as far as possible. Notice how far out your arm extends. Now, try the same movement again, only this time allowing your shoulder line to rotate left as you extend your right arm. Notice how much extra extension you can get using torso rotation. Now unwind at the torso and see how much of the forward stroke you can do before you bend your arm. The torso element of the stroke is 50 percent stronger than the arms element.

Practice your forward stroke with the torso rotation by looking down at where your life jacket hits your spray skirt. Your

FIG. 2 **Plant blade at the toes . . .**

FIG. 3 **out at the hips.**

life jacket should rotate 45 degrees in each direction with each stroke. Don't focus on how much your shoulders move back and forth, because this is not an accurate measure.

Most people, even when they are using the torso twist only, use only half of the twist in their stroke. Your goal is to get your next stroke in the water as fast as possible after your last one came out (at the hip). Since your body is a spring, it will begin to unwind the instant you take your paddle out of the water. If you hesitate before putting your next stroke in the water, you will unwind halfway before it gets in the water and will not be using the spring in your muscles to pull the paddle, thus reducing the effectiveness of the torso twist.

FIG. 4 **Torso wound up . . .**

FIG. 5 **torso unwinding . . .**

FIG. 6 **torso wound up again.**

BOAT POSITION AND MOVEMENT

Don't allow the boat to rock from side to side. Though the boat will always yaw slightly, keep it as flat as possible when paddling forward by using a good vertical stroke, in at the toe, out at the hip. The boat should remain dead flat.

FORWARD STROKE REVIEW

LEVEL 1

- Body position is forward.
- Grip is following the 90-degree rule, straight wrist on noncontrol hand.
- Paddle goes in at the toes, out at the hip.
- Top hand pushes down along the axis of the shaft, not punching forward.
- Torso twist is at the waist, 45 degrees each way on each stroke.
- Quick transition between strokes.
- Boat is quiet, no rocking side to side.

Once you are paddling within the parameters above, you are ready to move on to the next level of awareness and focus on additional fine-tuning skills.

LEVEL 2

- Feel the water on the blades with each stroke, and don't let it slip off the sides. Keep the blade square to the water. You should feel the resistance of the water when pulling.
- Feel the boat jump forward the moment the paddle enters the water, and maximize it with the torso twist and a solid, quick plant of the paddle.
- Add to the drill several ten-stroke sprints, at full speed, and maintain proper technique.
- Paddle the boat holding an edge in the water (30 degree lean) without rocking.

Once you are paddling consistently at levels 1 and 2, you are ready to move on to the next level and focus on applying these techniques and awareness to whitewater.

LEVEL 3

- Practice your forward stroke during ferries, through wave trains, and on attainments, with the focus on the techniques of level 1 and the awareness of level 2. Feel the characteristics of the water: boils, eddylines, depth, and aeration during each stroke. This will help you build awareness of your stroke effectiveness, whatever the water is doing. Practice controlling the rate at which you pull through the water, based on the characteristics of both the water your blade is in and the water available for your next stroke. Focus on the basic techniques for levels 1 and 2 while adjusting for the whitewater. Congratulations. You have completed the first section of the warm-up drills.

STROKE	Reverse Stroke
DRILL	Take 60 reverse strokes: 30 slow, 15 medium, 15 fast
GOALS	To be able to paddle as comfortably in reverse as forward and to increase awareness of where you are and where you're going when in reverse. Also, to warm up the front shoulder muscles and prevent muscle imbalance

When you watch beginners try to paddle forward in a straight line, you see them constantly correcting. They usually learn to paddle straight without the correction strokes in a few outings. Can you paddle in reverse without correction strokes? Seventy-five percent or more of the kayakers out there can't. This means that they are at the beginner level of paddling backward. The inability to paddle backward comfortably in a straight line is a real handicap for all types of whitewater paddling. Reverse strokes are simple; but developing awareness while moving backward requires practice.

Focus on the techniques below during the sixty strokes above and, ultimately, on every reverse stroke you take. A good reverse stroke (Fig. 7–9) improves your ability to backferry and to backsurf and is a vital component of many other moves.

A good reverse stroke has three important elements: proper paddle position and movement, proper body position and movement, and proper boat position and movement.

PADDLE POSITION AND MOVEMENT

The paddle goes in the water just behind the butt and comes out just in front of the knee
- This keeps the paddle within the power range.
- It also keeps your arms and body in a stable position.

The paddle is nearly vertical, the more vertical, the better
- This maximizes efficiency and control.
- A vertical paddle is the most effective. It pulls the boat straight backward without causing it to yaw. A boat that doesn't yaw goes faster and stays in control.

- Start the top hand high, over the centerline of the boat, and keep it on the same side as your stroke. If you keep the top hand low, the paddle strokes will be sweeps that push the boat sideways as well as backward. Keep your paddle shaft next to the boat so that you are pushing the boat straight back.

BODY POSITION AND MOVEMENT
By keeping your body forward, you keep the back edges from catching, you are ready for your next move, and you are practicing the same techniques you will need for backsurfing and back ferries.

BOAT POSITION AND MOVEMENT

Most boaters get lost in a hurry when they start going backward. The problem is small in flatwater but compounds quickly once you hit whitewater. This lack of awareness of boat position is most apparent when you try to peel out backward onto a wave or backferry at a specific spot. Your goat is to know where you are and where you are going and to be able to make small corrections along the way.

FIG. 7   **Torso wound up, preparing to plant blade, looking at target . . .**

FIG. 8   **use a vertical stroke . . .**

FIG. 9 **out in front of knees.**

REVERSE STROKE REVIEW

LEVEL 1

- Body position is forward.
- Paddle is as vertical as possible.
- Paddle goes in behind butt, out in front of knees.
- Boat is flat, not rocking side to side.
- Look over shoulder every three to five strokes.
- Know where you are and where you are going at all times.

Once you are paddling within the parameters above, you are ready to move on to the next level of awareness and focus on additional fine-tuning skills.

LEVEL 2

- Do the reverse stroke drill in moving water and going across small eddylines, still going from point A to point B with as few correction strokes as possible.
- Paddle the boat holding an edge in the water (30 degree lean), still with no rocking.

LEVEL 3

- Do the last fifteen strokes of the reverse stroke drill at full speed and in waves, moving downriver, and know where you are and where you are going at all times.

Primary Turning Strokes

Before we begin discussing the specific primary turning strokes, concepts, and drills, there is one general rule you need to make a habit of as you work to refine your turning stroke techniques.

HEAD AND BODY LEAD EVERY TURN

- Look where you are going. It is imperative that you have your eyes fixed on your target at all times. A common mistake is to look over your bow or at the paddle on sweep strokes.
- This is the most effective position for your body to assist in turning the boat. If your body is pointed at the target, your boat will try to catch up, because the spring action in your muscles tries to get your legs caught up with your torso.
- It puts your body in position for the next stroke. If you have your body squared up or aiming the wrong way, such as looking at your paddle on sweep strokes, you are in the worst possible position to take your next stroke. Leading with the head and body is as important to turning as hip snapping is to rolling. You must lead your boat with your head and body if you expect to control your turns. Controlling your turns is a vital element of playboating, slalom racing, and running difficult creeks and rivers.

Let's begin with the forward sweep technique. Although it is extremely simple and most first-timers can do it perfectly, the forward sweep stroke has been taught incorrectly in practically every book, video, class, and instructor training course for the past twenty years. The result has been devastating to boaters.

STROKE   Forward Sweep

DRILL   10 forward sweeps

GOALS   To make leading your boat with your head and body
          habitual and to warm up your back and torso

EXERCISE Sit up in a chair. Keep your knees pointed
          straight ahead. Now turn your head and your
          body as far to the left as they go. Try to look
          behind you. You should not stop turning until
          your body prevents you from going any farther.
          This is leading your left turn with your head
          and body. Do the same for a right turn

Focus on the techniques below during these ten strokes and, ultimately, on every forward sweep stroke you take. A good forward sweep (Fig. 10–12) improves your ability to turn your boat with control and intent.

The three elements to a good forward sweep are: proper paddle position and movement, proper body position and movement, and proper boat position and movement.

PADDLE POSITION AND MOVEMENT

- The paddle goes in at the toes and comes out at the hip. Your objective is to push the bow away from the paddle.
- The stroke starts with the paddle as parallel to the side of the boat as possible. This requires that your nonpower hand be at nose level or lower. Your objective is maximum rotation of the boat during the stroke without sacrificing control or putting yourself in an awkward position.
- You want to push the paddle as far from the boat as you can without unwinding the torso.
- Pull the paddle out at the hip. If you sweep the paddle past the hip, you are doing a poor stern draw, not a forward sweep.

FIG. 10   Lead with head and body . . .

BODY POSITION AND MOVEMENT

- Your body should be fully rotated in the direction of the turn. Your head should be rotated far enough to see your stern.
- You should keep your body wound up and still during the sweeps.
- Do not unwind to get more power.

At first glance, it makes sense to use torso rotation during the sweep to add power to the stroke. Watching the paddle forces you to add torso rotation to the sweep. You can see why this technique has been taught for twenty years. Well, welcome to the new millennium: Let's catch up with the times.

BOAT POSITION AND MOVEMENT

- Your boat should spin in a circle quickly when you do your ten sweeps. Avoid rocking the boat from side to side.
- Hold your boat steady to learn edge control. When you focus on keeping the boat flat, you learn to have active strokes but a quiet body and boat. If your boat rocks from side to side while you do multiple sweep strokes, you have an edge control problem. This problem will become apparent on strong eddy-lines, when squirting, wavespinning, or cartwheeling. If you are a slalom boater you will have problems on eddylines, in upstreams, back ferries, and pivot turns.

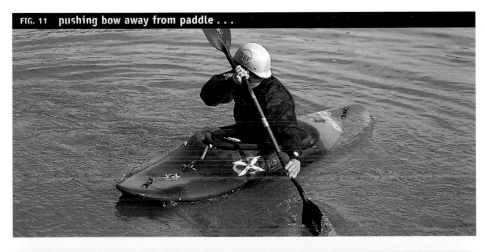

FIG. 11 **pushing bow away from paddle . . .**

FIG. 12 **paddle out before stern, boat stays flat.**

FORWARD SWEEP REVIEW

LEVEL 1

- Head and body are wound up as much as physically possible.
- Paddle goes in at the toes, nearly parallel to the length of the boat.
- Top hand is in front of your nose.
- Push the bow away from the paddle and continue the sweep to the hip.

- Head and body remain wound up during the stroke.
- Keep boat float with no rocking.
- Keep looking over stern.

Once the above elements of your sweep stroke are habitual, you have taken a giant step toward solid basics and are ready to progress to the next level.

LEVEL 2

- Practice your sweeps while leaning the boat to the inside of the turn. Choose an angle (30 degrees is good), and hold it steady while sweeping in circles.
- Practice your sweeps while leaning the boat to the outside also, again about 30 degrees.
- Do your sweeps at different speeds and intensities to get a feel for the boat's spinning ability.
- Feel also the effect of having your body wound and your ability to have a higher stroke rate than with the old school sweep.

- Practice pushing the paddle far from the boat, and also close to the boat as in a forward stroke.
- Combine your forward and reverse sweeps together in one drill, doing ten forward and ten reverse sweeps in each direction. (See Reverse Sweep Stroke before doing this.)
- When you are comfortable with the boat leans and combining the forward and reverse sweeps together, then you can move on to the level 3 drill.

LEVEL 3

- If you have a boat with a squirtable stern or bow, you can practice advanced edge control while doing your warm-up sweep drills.

- Lean your boat 30 degrees to the inside of the turn and practice pushing the bow edge underwater as much as possible. You need sharp strokes, solid edge control, and forward posture. Keep the bow going under on each stroke, and keep the stroke rate high.

- Do the same with an outside lean. Push the stern under with your sweep stroke. You need to have a neutral body position to make this work. Keep the sweeps coming quickly.

Congratulations. You have completed the third section of the warm-up drills.

STROKE	Reverse Sweep
DRILL	10 reverse sweeps on each side
GOALS	To learn powerful, effective reverse sweeps, and to warm up your torso

Do ten reverse sweeps on one side before doing the ten sweeps on the other side. Remember that the forward and reverse sweeps are the primary turning strokes. The reverse sweep (Fig. 13–14) is a very powerful stroke that spins the boat faster than any other stroke. It is also the stroke you use to squirt your stern and stop the boat to reverse direction. It can be done many different ways, but it is critical to learn it in its pure and most effective form first. Once you have the reverse sweep down in its pure form, you can shorten the stroke, change the position of the paddle, or use it in combination with other strokes.

There are three elements to the reverse sweep: proper paddle position and movement, proper body position and movement, and proper boat position and movement.

PADDLE POSITION AND MOVEMENT

- The paddle goes in at the stern and comes out at the knees.
- Your back arm should be straight.
- Your paddle blade should touch the stern.
- You will be using the back face of the paddle blade against the water.
- Your paddle shaft should start parallel to the side of the boat.
- You should be looking at the stern and see the paddle blade enter the water.

Now you are ready to
take your reverse sweep

- Push the stern away from the paddle blade, keeping your back arm straight.
- Carry the stroke out and away from the boat until your blade is even with your knees.
- Pull the stroke out even with your knees.

BODY POSITION AND MOVEMENT

- Your torso should be fully rotated when the blade goes in the water.
- You should see your stern.
- Keep your body vertical and over the boat; avoid leaning back.
- Keep your torso wound up during the stroke as you would with a forward sweep.

BOAT POSITION AND MOVEMENT

- Your boat should spin quickly with each stroke.
- Keep the boat flat; avoid any rocking back and forth. As with the forward strokes, focusing on keeping the boat from rocking while doing your sweeps will teach you edge control.

Most people have fairly good reverse sweeps. The most common mistakes are a lack of extension on the back arm and too much rocking of the boat.

FIG. 13   Back arm straight, paddle in at stern . . .

FIG. 14   out at knees.

REVERSE SWEEP REVIEW

LEVEL 1

- Keep body upright.
- Watch paddle enter water at stern (touching the stern).
- Keep back arm straight.
- Use back face of paddle against water.
- Stroke starts at stern and ends at knees.

- Keep boat from rocking side to side while doing your sweeps.

Once you can do the reverse sweeps with a quiet boat and fully extended arm, you are ready for the next level, which involves putting the forward and reverse sweeps together.

LEVEL 2

- Combine your forward and reverse sweeps during your warm-up. This allows you to focus on keeping your torso rotated, and getting in twice as many strokes in about the same time. Your technique will be the same for each stroke.

- Practice one-third of your strokes leaning to the outside of the turn, one-third of the strokes leaning to the inside of the turn, and one-third of the strokes keeping the boat flat (twenty one strokes total in each direction). Do not allow the lean of the boat to vary during the strokes; hold your angle steady.

LEVEL 3

- If you have a boat with a squirtable bow or stern, try to keep your edge underwater during the process of doing your sweeps. Your stern edge will be underwater while leaning to the outside, and the bow edge will go underwater while leaning to the inside.

You can now do forward and reverse sweeps. Remember that these strokes are your first and last lines of defense for turning your kayak. If you are lazy in developing your sweeps, you will not have a fully effective sweep when you need one to avoid trouble or get where you want to go. If, for example, you do a reverse sweep without putting your paddle at the stern and having full body rotation, your stroke may lose 30 percent or more effectiveness. Unless you've practiced the strokes in their proper form during your warm-ups, you won't be able to use perfect technique when you need it. Practice the easy strokes with as much diligence as the more complex ones.

Secondary Turning Strokes

This next section isn't as easy as the previous ones in terms of the concepts and habits you likely need to overcome. This section offers several concepts, rules, and strokes, all of which work together to make you infinitely more effective and efficient. All of the strokes and concepts are easy; however, there is no point at which you will have thoroughly mastered them. It is an ongoing learning process that will challenge you for as long as you strive to improve.

The first concept we will address is spin momentum, a factor that affects everything you do in a kayak.

SPIN MOMENTUM

Kayaks are unique craft in that they are not designed to go straight. In fact, most new kayaks are specifically designed to turn as easily as possible, with no consideration to tracking. Something interesting happens when you get a kayak moving forward or backward: The kayak wants to spin out in one direction or the other. Every beginner has fought spin momentum when trying to paddle in a straight line and most beginners are unable to keep the boat going straight. Kayaks try to convert your forward speed into spin momentum. No matter how straight you think you're going, if you stop paddling, the boat will instantly start to spin out and won't stop spinning until the boat has lost its speed. This force, called spin momentum, is annoying to a beginner, but when properly harnessed, it sets the expert kayaker free.

Some facts about spin momentum: It exists every moment you have attained any speed with your kayak. The faster you are moving, the more forceful the spin momentum. You either control spin momentum or are a slave to it. You should now understand spin momentum, at least from a theoretical point of view.

RULES FOR TURNING A KAYAK

Rule 1: *Your head and body should lead the boat in every turn* (sound familiar?).

Rule 2: *Always control your turns with strokes on the inside of the turn.* What exactly does that mean? If you want to turn left, you should first get the boat spinning left with a sweep; then you control the radius of the turn, your forward speed, how much you slide sideways—everything—with your left blade. Your right blade is useless except for forward strokes to help keep the boat speed up. The reverse is true for a right turn.

Rule 3: *Always use a draw stroke to control your turn.*

The draw, often referred to as the "dufek," is the most misunderstood and misused stroke in kayaking. Learning the draw as it is presented in the next section will significantly improve your paddling skills.

Let's get to it.

There are three elements to a good draw: proper paddle position and movement, proper body position and movement, and proper boat position and movement. You first need to understand what your goals are when doing a draw.

- To control your turn.
- To convert your forward momentum from one direction to another.
- To harness spin momentum.
- To harness the river's energy.

A draw is to your kayak what a keel is to a sailboat. A sailboat doesn't work without a keel, and a kayak doesn't work well without one either. The job of a keel is to keep a boat from sliding sideways. A kayak is extremely inefficient in turning, because it slides and loses all of its speed, unless you use your paddle as a keel. Then it doesn't matter what design you are paddling, you can carve turns efficiently.

On a sailboat, the keel goes at the center of longitudinal buoyancy—the middle of the boat. A draw stroke likewise should be done at the middle of the kayak. This is contradictory to what is taught elsewhere.

PADDLE POSITION AND MOVEMENT

For the draw stroke, there are three paddle blade angles you can use: normal position, open-face position, and closed-face position.

Normal Position

Put the paddle in at your hip in the draw position, keeping the blade parallel to the side of the boat so that if you were moving forward, the blade would be slicing through the water with no resistance. (Fig. 15)

Open-Face Position

Starting in the normal position on the right side of your boat, rotate your paddle shaft clockwise about 30 degrees so that the leading edge of the paddle blade is farther from the kayak than the trailing edge. This is an open face. The same goes for the left draw, only rotate it counterclockwise. (Fig. 16)

Closed-Face Position

Starting in the draw position on the right side of the boat, rotate your paddle shaft counterclockwise about 30 degrees. This is a closed-face position. (Fig. 17)

BODY POSITION AND MOVEMENT

Keep your body forward and rotated in the direction of the turn. The sharper you need to turn the more you will need to rotate your body.

BOAT POSITION AND MOVEMENT

See the Review Section of the draw stroke for boat positions to use in different situations.

PRACTICING DRAWS

• Grab a paddle and sit in a chair.
• Hold the paddle with your right hand only, and put the paddle one foot from the side of your right hip.
• Hold the paddle there and make it totally vertical.

FIG. 15 **Normal face.**

FIG. 16 **Open face.**

FIG. 17 **Closed face.**

- Now face the paddle shaft, looking in the direction of your turn.
- Rotate your head and body to face the paddle.
- Reach over with your left hand and grab the shaft.

This is a draw. (Fig. 18–19)

Now look at where your blade is: Oops, you've moved it forward already; get it back to your hip.

- Now, while keeping the blade 1 foot from where the side of the boat would be and vertical, move the paddle up to your knees; this is a bow draw. (Fig. 20)
- Now move the paddle back 1 foot behind your butt and vertical; this is a stern draw. (Fig. 21) (Is your paddle vertical on the stern draw? It should be.)

The next thing you need to look at is your blade angle. Remember that you are creating a keel with your paddle. What does a keel look like? It is parallel to the boat and vertical. So forget what you may have thought a draw was supposed to be, and make sure your paddle is vertical, at your butt, and that the blade is perfectly parallel to the boat. Now you have a keel for your kayak. The draw stroke is incredibly versatile and effective because you can use many different positions and angles to maximize the effect you want. Applications to whitewater are discussed later. For now, you need to learn to make the boat glide and to convert your forward momentum from one direction to another using the draw.

Let's do a quick review before actually putting the draw to use in flatwater.

CRITICAL ELEMENTS OF THE DRAW

Common mistake: putting paddle in at the knee, or even slightly in front of center of gravity.

FIG. 18   **Normal draw position.**

FIG. 19   **Head and body face paddle.**

FIG. 20 **Bow draw.**

FIG. 21 **Stern draw.**

Proper technique: paddle blade must be at or slightly behind your center of gravity—your butt.

Common mistake: holding the paddle at an angle by keeping top arm over boat. If your paddle is at 45 degrees, then half of your energy is lifting the boat up and half is keeping the boat from slipping. So if you are putting 20 pounds of pressure on the paddle, only 10 pounds are actually helping your turn. Thus, a vertical paddle is the only way to go.

Proper technique: paddle must be vertical. (Fig. 22)

Common mistake: opening up the blade angle so that the paddle acts as a brake instead of a keel. Almost 99 percent of all draws are done with an open-face paddle blade that is not vertical. If you saw a sailboat with a keel that was near the bow, leaning over at a 45-degree angle and rotated out 45 degrees, you would say that keel was clearly broken and nonfunctional.

Proper technique: paddle blade must be parallel to the boat—or closed-face.

USING THE DRAW STROKE

Forgetting everything you have learned so far about the draw stroke, grab a friend and try this test on the water: Have your friend face you and put his paddle on his deck so that it makes a right angle with the side of his boat. Now paddle past his right blade, make a tight turn around his boat, and continue past the left blade on the other side of his boat. Your goal is to use the minimum number of strokes. Start counting the strokes when you cross the right blade, and stop counting when you cross the left blade. The average number of strokes is four to five. It is impossible to do it in fewer than three without using some kind of draw stroke.

Now do the same test again, this time using the proper draw position. Remember that the draw only acts as a keel to keep your boat from sliding while it turns; it is not a primary turning stroke. Paddle up to your friend's paddle, making your last stroke before you reach him a sweep to initiate the turn. Immediately put the draw in the normal position and glide around the stern of his boat. Now slice your paddle forward to the bow and pull yourself forward. If you do it properly, you will be able to make the entire maneuver in one stroke. You will also have more forward speed when you cross the finish line than you did with four or five strokes the old way. Wow!

Every turn you do without a proper draw stroke forces you to use four to five times the number of strokes and it takes more time to do it. This is not only inefficient but also dangerous when you need to make a move that includes a turn in it. You can learn to do in one stroke what your friends do in five; that is worth the effort.

You have now seen what a difference a draw makes in your paddling. If you didn't notice any major difference, you are still making one of two mistakes:

- You are putting the draw in front of your butt. No matter how many times you read that the draw must go in at your butt or slightly behind, you will be tempted to put it in too far in front and not realize it. You will see no progress until you get your paddle at or behind your butt.
- You are using an open-face position. This is a braking stroke that kills your momentum. You might as well drop an anchor.

To apply the draw stroke to your everyday paddling, remember one important rule for turning a kayak: Always control the turn with strokes on the inside of the turn. The stroke for controlling all turns is a draw stroke. There is only one way to propel the boat on the inside of the turn, and that is with a C-stroke, a compound stroke that combines a short bow draw with a forward stroke.

FIG 22 **Use vertical paddle, face paddle.**

STROKE	**C-stroke**
DRILL	**One large circle and one small circle in each direction, 10 strokes in a straight line, paddling on one side only**
GOALS	**To learn how to control your turns using the draw and to master spin momentum in flatwater so that you can apply it to whitewater**

There are three elements of the C-stroke to learn: proper paddle position and movement, proper body position and movement, and proper boat position and movement.

PADDLE POSITION AND MOVEMENT

Keeping in mind that your goals are to control your turn and to propel your boat forward, start with a bow draw (vertical draw at your knees). Pull the draw towards your knees until the paddle shaft touches the boat, then convert the stroke into a forward stroke, keeping the paddle vertical. The blade should be closed-face during the draw portion of the C-stroke to assist in pulling the boat forward. This is a full-scale C-stroke. (Fig. 23–26) Technically, you can call any stroke on the inside of the turn a C-stroke, or at least it should be.

The C-stroke requires that you are moving forward and have spin momentum. This stroke is used every time you are paddling forward and turning. The paddle position and movement depend on how tight of a turn you want to make. To make a tight turn, use more bow draw before converting to a forward stroke. To make a wide turn, use very little or no draw before the forward stroke.

BODY POSITION AND MOVEMENT

Keep your body forward and rotated in the direction of the turn. The sharper you need to turn, the more you will need to rotate your body.

BOAT POSITION AND MOVEMENT

Keep the boat flat while learning the stroke and then practice with inside and outside boat leans to develop edge control.

FIG. 23 Closed-face bow draw . . .

FIG. 24 vertical forward stroke . . .

FIG. 25 out at hips.

FIG. 26 Repeat with closed-face bow draw.

C-STROKE REVIEW

LEVEL 1

- You should be able to paddle in a circle with only forward strokes on the inside of the turn.
- You should be able to do a bow draw at your knees and convert that stroke into a forward stroke, all while moving forward and turning in the direction of your paddle.

- You should be able to do a series of C-strokes and control the radius of your turn. If you don't overpower your spin momentum you can paddle in circles forever using C-strokes.
- Keep your paddle vertical at all times.
- The paddle goes in at the knees and out at the hip.

LEVEL 2

- Use a closed-face paddle during the bow draw, which will force the boat to move forward when you pull your draw into your knees.
- Practice getting your paddle blade actually under the boat for a past-vertical C-stroke. This allows you to keep turning even when you pull on the paddle, and it is a little overcompensation exercise that gets you in the habit of keeping the blade vertical.

- Practice starting with a stationary boat and getting your boat moving and spinning using C-strokes (spinning toward your paddle). This will take some careful strokes.
- Practice doing your big circle while keeping your boat on its inside edge (about 30 degrees) the entire time. Be sure not to lean on your paddle.

LEVEL 3

- Practice opening up the radius of the turn so far that you are practically going straight. Keep a small amount of spin momentum to allow you to stroke on one side. Don't overpower your spin momentum. This drill is like walking a tightrope; It requires a good understanding of spin momentum and the ability to do C-strokes.
- Practice doing C-strokes with current and eddylines. You should be able to keep the boat moving and turning, no matter what currents you hit. Watch the current so that you know how much of a draw you need.

STROKE	S-turn
DRILL	20 turns, 10 to each side
GOALS	To learn how to convert your spin momentum from one direction to another and how to glide on the draw using the S-turn stroke drill, to learn how to do compound strokes effectively, to be able to do quick transfers from one stroke to another, and to improve paddle dexterity through feathering and compound strokes

The S-turn is a compound stroke that is a combination of a draw, slice to bow, and sweep. You need to understand what you are trying to achieve with this drill before you try to learn it. You have learned how to start the boat turning with a sweep and how to keep the boat moving forward while turning with the draw, but not how to straighten out or turn the other way. The S-turn stroke sequence is just that: the most effective way to turn left, then back to the right, and then left again, all the while keeping the boat moving forward. This is the equivalent of a skier slaloming down the mountain versus traversing from one side of the slope to the other. If you have ever skied, you should appreciate the importance of linking turns together. You should use the S-turn stroke in some form every time you make a maneuver that has two or more turns in it, which is often.

A good S-turn has the same three elements as every other stroke; proper paddle position and movement, proper boat position and movement, and proper body position and movement, but here, to avoid confusion, you need to consider the boat position and movement first.

BOAT POSITION AND MOVEMENT

Imagine a skier slaloming down a slope, cutting back and forth yet keeping her momentum downward. You would expect good skiers to make smooth, flowing turns, using their edges to carve the turns instead of sliding and keeping their forward momentum going from top to bottom. Now imagine the same movement in a kayak on flatwater. This is the boat movement you are looking for in the S-turn drill. For learning purposes, keep your boat flat and your weight over the boat.

PADDLE POSITION AND MOVEMENT

There are three elements of the S-turn for your paddle:
- Normal position or slightly closed-face draw.
- Feathering your paddle from the draw position to the forward sweep position.
- Forward sweep.

You already know each element of the S-turn stroke except the feathering part from previous stroke drills (see Draw Stroke and Forward Sweep). This leaves only feathering to learn before you can S-turn.

Feathering

Feathering is simply slicing your paddle through the water like a dorsal fin on a shark. The most common form of feathering is slicing your paddle parallel towards your boat, from your butt to your toes and back. The benefit behind feathering your paddle through the water versus taking it out and putting it back in where you want it is *control*. You have maximum control over your boat when your paddle is in the water. Every moment you have your paddle out of the water you are at the mercy of many forces that can make you lose control of your boat.

To practice feathering, put your paddle in the normal draw position (see Draw Stroke). Now slice, or feather, your paddle back and forth from your butt to your toes over and over again. Your objective is to keep the blade about 6 inches from the boat and following a straight line. Normal difficulties with feathering are losing control of the blade and hitting the side of the boat. Some paddles are designed better than others for feathering. The best paddles have no rib on the back face and feather straight. Once you can feather from your butt to your toes quickly ten times, you are ready to continue with the S-turn drill. (Fig. 27–32)

Here is the stroke sequence in its entirety:

- Paddle forward to get some speed.
- Do a forward sweep to get the boat spinning (just a little spin momentum).
- Put your normal draw in immediately on the other side at your hip, and let the boat turn and glide until it has turned 45 degrees. To prevent overturning, get your draw in faster and farther behind your butt.
- Feather your paddle up to your toes from the draw position to the forward sweep position.
- Rotate your head and body, and do a forward sweep to make the boat spin the other way.
- Repeat the last three steps.

Visualize a skier coming down a slope, S-turning and moving forward the whole time. That's what you want to look like in your boat. A common mistake is to overturn the boat so that it zigzags too much and has no forward momentum. This is a result of one or more of the following: not starting with any forward speed; waiting too long to put your draw in after you do your sweep; putting your draw in front of your butt (center of gravity). Remember that your goal when you do your draw is to control your turn and keep the boat moving. The boat will turn from its spin momentum faster than you want it to, so you must control the turn by using a stern draw just barely behind your butt.

BODY POSITION AND MOVEMENT

Keep your body weight over the boat at all times. Your head and body should face the paddle during the draw; lead every turn with your head and body. When you feather your paddle from your draw to your sweep position, you are preparing to turn the boat the other way, so start rotating your head and body away from your paddle blade for your sweep. Keep a quiet body when doing the drill; you don't want your torso to be moving forward and backward. Now you have the information to do an effective S-turn.

FIG. 27 Forward sweep on left . . .

FIG. 28 transition . . .

FIG. 29 normal draw on right . . .

FIG. 30   **feather paddle to bow rotate body left . . .**

FIG. 31   **forward sweep on right . . .**

FIG. 32   **normal draw on left.**

S-TURN REVIEW

LEVEL 1

- Paddle forward to get speed.
- Do a forward sweep to get the boat spinning (just a little spin).
- Throw in a normal draw on the opposite side immediately following the sweep.
- Let the boat glide until you have turned 45 degrees from your original direction of travel.
- Feather your paddle to your toes, and rotate your head and body for your next turn.
- Do a forward sweep to change the direction of your spin momentum and to get the boat spinning the other direction.

- Repeat the steps.

Things to look for:
- Boat moving forward and gliding during your draws.
- Reversing your spin momentum with your sweep.

Things to avoid:
- Overspinning and stalling.
- Big body or boat leans.
- Trying to turn the boat with a bow draw.

LEVEL 2

- Begin the draw with a C-stroke before your draw to improve forward speed.
- Glide for three to five seconds on each draw, without losing any forward speed by putting pressure on the draw near the stern, thus a closed-face stern draw.
- Practice in moving water while watching the little currents and boils to help you turn and glide.

LEVEL 3

- Practice while paddling downstream in waves, trying to time the strokes to accelerate off the waves.
- Practice crossing eddies in the middle of the river using the S-turn sequence. You should be able to glide all the way across the eddy on your draw. (See S-turns in the Whitewater section.)
- Practice taking two or more C-strokes in between each sweep to give yourself more crosscurrent travel for each turn.

STROKE	**Offside C-stroke**
DRILL	**10 strokes in a wide turn,**
	4 strokes in a tight turn to each side
GOALS	**To increase paddle dexterity, to learn to paddle with one blade, to improve spin momentum awareness, and to stretch out back and shoulders**

Now you will be doing the first stroke that seems, at first, like a total waste of time and effort. That's OK; everything is not as it seems, and you won't truly appreciate what some of your new skills will do for you immediately. You'll have to trust me on some of the skills and drills you'll be learning next. The offside C-stroke is the same as your normal C-stroke, except that your paddle is on the wrong side of the boat. C-1s and open canoes have to use offside C-strokes to paddle effectively without switching hands.

Let me first offer you some motivation to practice offside C-strokes. Can you paddle an entire river using a broken paddle? With an offside C-stroke you can. You won't have to switch hands in the middle of rapids, either. Do you have a complete stroke repertoire and strong paddle dexterity? You don't without an effective offside C-stroke.

That should be enough explanation to get you started. Let's learn our paddle position and movement, body position and movement, and boat position and movement.

PADDLE POSITION AND MOVEMENT

Using your right blade, set up a normal draw on the left side of your boat. You will be reaching across your body, so this position may seem awkward at first. Keep a vertical paddle and blade at the butt and just a few inches from the boat. Now open the face 30 degrees, and feather the paddle up to your knees and away from the boat. Pull the blade toward your knees, and then convert the paddle face to a forward stroke, pulling the blade back to your butt, then repeat. (Fig. 33–36) Your paddle will make a pie-shaped wedge. Your objective is to keep the boat moving forward and turning toward your paddle. This means you need forward speed to start and spin momentum toward the side on which you want to do your strokes. From the beginning, it goes like this:

- Paddle forward to get some speed, then do a sweep on the right to get the boat spinning left.
- Immediately put your right blade in at your knees on the left side of the boat, and pull yourself forward with an offside forward stroke.
- Once your blade is back to your butt, feather it forward and away from the boat to get it in a bow draw position on your off side.
- Pull your blade to your knees and then back to your butt, which both turns the boat and pulls it forward.
- Repeat ten times on each side. This is your offside C-stroke.

FIG. 33 Blade in draw position . . .

FIG. 34 open face to feather . . .

FIG. 35 feather to bow . . .

FIG. 36 pull boat forward.

Common mistakes:
- No forward speed or spin momentum before starting.
- Letting the boat spin out immediately and losing all of the forward speed and spin momentum before getting the first stroke in.
- Using all draw and no forward stroke, so that the boat turns a lot but stops moving forward.
- Using all forward stroke but no draw, so that you overpower the spin momentum and turn the wrong way.
- Not keeping pressure on the blade the entire time.

BODY POSITION AND MOVEMENT
- Your body should be forward and over the boat.

The flatwater offside C-stroke drill you are doing should have a focus on several things:
1. Keeping the forward speed.
   - Start with forward speed.
   - Keep the spin momentum to a minimum when you do your forward sweep to spin the boat.
   - Pull fairly hard on the forward stroke and right along the edge of the boat.
   - Punch with the top hand until it is almost straight. (This is a great stretch for the back, too.)

2. Keep the spin momentum going in the right direction.
   - Don't overpower the spin momentum by pulling too hard or too far from the boat.
   - Watch the boat during all aspects of the stroke and make sure it's always spinning the right direction. You'll know how much draw you need and how much forward stroke you can take based on how much spin momentum you have.
3. Control the radius of the turn.
   - Your goal with this stroke drill is to be able to control the boat on the off side. You need to practice making large circles and small circles by adjusting your draw and forward stroke. Remember that more draw at the bow means more turn, while more forward stroke means less turn.

BOAT POSITION AND MOVEMENT
- Keep your boat flat during the exercise, and keep your weight over the boat for maximum control and balance. Your boat should go in a circle during the ten strokes with a radius that you determine by setting the amount of draw and the amount of forward pull that you do with each stroke.

OFFSIDE C-STROKE REVIEW

LEVEL 1

- You should be able to paddle forward and in circles, using only one blade on the opposite side of the boat from where it normally goes in.
- Your paddle movement is to feather out, draw in to your knees, then pull your boat forward. Think "Out and forward, In, Pull . . . Out and forward, In, Pull." That is your motion.
- You should be able to do ten strokes in a row keeping the boat moving in a wide circle, and then four strokes tightening the turn up very small.
- Punching with the top hand helps with forward speed during the forward stroke part.
- Feathering out and away from the boat helps control the boat, turn it, and set up the draw.
- Flexibility of your torso and shoulders will improve by doing this stroke.

LEVEL 2

- Practice in an eddy by crossing the eddyline and going back into the eddy and then back out again, using only offside C-strokes.
- Try to use the current when you peel out to help with spin momentum and allow you to pull harder to accelerate the boat.
- Practice going in and out of eddies on the off side when river running, remembering the rules for draws and applying them to the draw part of the offside C-stroke.

LEVEL 3

- Try to paddle in a circle so wide that you are almost going straight on the off side.
- If you are paddling a boat that squirts, practice squirting the boat on an eddyline using offside C-strokes.
- Paddle entire rapids on one blade only, catching eddies and ferrying on the off side. Practice using both left and right offside C-strokes.
- Be able to control your boat so well on the off side that you are comfortable with stern draws, river running, hitting holes, surfing waves, and so forth, all using one blade.

STROKE	Reverse Compound Stroke
DRILL	One large and one small circle in each direction
GOALS	To effectively control the boat backward with one blade, to improve feathering and controlling the spin momentum of the boat while feathering, and to improve backward paddling ability

By learning to paddle backward using the reverse compound stroke, you are opening up many new possibilities in your paddling. You will be able to exit an eddy backward for a ferry, surf a wave, or peel out with confidence and control. Backward paddling will become much more common in your general river running and playing, because it will become so much easier.

PADDLE POSITION AND MOVEMENT

There are two components to the reverse compound stroke. There is the *catch,* when your paddle enters the water at your stern and you begin to pull yourself backward. Then you *flip* the blade over, while it stays at your hip, and finish the stroke with a normal backstroke to your toes. The second part of the stroke is a simple backstroke and shouldn't confuse you; however, pay attention to the first part.

- Reach back and put your paddle in at the stern, power face down (spoon part facing the water). (Fig. 37)
- Keep your top hand at eye level.
- Rotate your body so you can see the paddle enter the water.

Now you are ready to pull the boat backward. (Fig. 38–41)

- Pull the paddle toward your butt and stop there.
- Flip the paddle face over 180 degrees so that you are in normal backstroke position.
- Push the paddle up to your knees.

The sequence goes like this: pull-flip-push, pull-flip-push. This stroke can be done like a typical backstroke, where you alternate between left and right strokes to go in a straight line backward. You should learn the mechanics of the stroke that way the first time you try it. However, the reverse compound stroke is designed for use with one blade in a circle, much like the C-stroke is for forward paddling and turning. You can't paddle in a circle with one blade unless you have speed and spin momentum toward the side you are paddling on. So make sure you paddle backward to get some speed and spin momentum before starting the reverse compound strokes.

You are now ready to add one more element of control to your reverse compound stroke: keeping your paddle in the water during the entire drill. This means you have to feather the paddle from your toes back to the stern in the transition between strokes. This is a good lesson in boat control and a perfect way to improve your paddle dexterity. When feathering back to the stern for the next stroke, you are able to control the radius of your turn and the amount of glide in between strokes. You are in the draw position while feathering and can apply blade pressure where needed.

BODY POSITION AND MOVEMENT

- Keep your body forward or neutral when reaching to the stern for the catch.
- Rotate your body so that you can see the blade enter the water at the stern.
- Keep your head and body facing the paddle shaft at all times.

BOAT POSITION AND MOVEMENT

- Keep your boat flat during the drill; avoid rocking.
- Your boat should be moving backward and turning toward your paddle at all times.
- Don't overpower your spin momentum, or you will end up in a flat spin and go nowhere.

FIG. 37 **Power face down for catch . . .**

FIG. 38 **pull with the power face . . .**

FIG. 39 **flip paddle around . . .**

FIG. 40 **finish with normal backstroke . . .**

FIG. 41 **feather back for next stroke.**

REVERSE COMPOUND STROKE REVIEW

LEVEL 1

- Get speed backward and spin momentum toward the side you want to paddle on first.
- Paddle goes in at stern, face down.
- Body is facing paddle, and you can see the blade enter the water.
- Pull paddle to your butt.

- Flip paddle over quickly, and then finish the stroke with a normal backstroke from butt to toes. Keep paddle close to boat.
- Feather paddle back to stern.
- Repeat.

LEVEL 2

- Same as Level 1, except focus on the radius of the turn. Control the radius by how hard you pull on the paddle during the stroke and by applying pressure to the blade when feathering back—near the bow to slow the turn or near the stern to quicken it.

- Practice gliding backward by holding the paddle in a normal or slightly bow draw position for a few seconds during the feather back to the stern. See how well you can keep the speed going without taking more strokes.

LEVEL 3

- Start your boat up from a dead stop by getting some spin momentum with a stern draw and going immediately into a reverse compound stroke. You shouldn't need to attain speed before starting if you are getting better at creating and keeping your spin momentum.

- Practice back ferries starting on the eddyline and using only the reverse compound stroke on the downstream side.
- Practice getting onto waves backward using only the reverse compound stroke. Don't rudder on the other side when you are on the wave; use a bow draw to keep from peeling off it, just like you did in flatwater.

STROKE	**Sideslip Stroke (Open-Face Stern Draw)**
DRILL	**Four sideslip strokes (two on each side), each of which you should continue until the initial forward momentum is gone**
GOALS	**To be able to pull your boat sideways while it is moving forward, using only an open-face stern draw; to learn to do lateral boat moves without turning; and to improve your understanding and feel for blade angles during draws**

If you can do the sideslip stroke, you won't need to turn your boat to go around obstacles. You will use it all of the time if you are playboating and getting on waves or into holes properly. To use this stroke, it is critical to have a feel for blade angle and draw position. You need to be able to move the draw toward the bow or stern and open and close the blade angle in the middle of the drill to keep the boat pointed straight ahead and slipping sideways.

PADDLE POSITION AND MOVEMENT

- The paddle position is an open-face stern draw (see Draw Stroke). Remember the basics for this draw.
- Paddle goes just behind your butt and is vertical.
- Head and body face the paddle.
- Blade is open-face (the edge closest to the bow is farthest from the side of the boat), never at more than 30 degrees of angle. Opening the blade up to 45 degrees or more makes it a brake that stops you.

BODY POSITION AND MOVEMENT

- Your body should be forward and facing the paddle.
- Keep your body stationary during the stroke.

BOAT POSITION AND MOVEMENT

- In flatwater, you need to have lots of forward speed before starting the stroke.
- Keep your boat dead flat during the drill. Your boat will be moving sideways and forward at the same time if you are doing it properly.

Now you are ready to do the sideslip stroke. Paddle forward with lots of speed, and make sure you have a little spin momentum toward the side you will do the stroke on. Put your open-face stern draw in the water, and pull the boat sideways. (Fig. 42–43) If your boat turns toward your paddle, you need to move the draw back toward the stern more. If your boat turns away from your paddle, you didn't have enough spin momentum toward the paddle when you started, or, you overpowered the spin momentum with your stern draw. The sideslip stroke is an active stroke that requires constant adjustment to keep the boat sliding and straight.

FIG. 42   Slightly open-face stern draw . . .

FIG. 43   pull boat sideways.

SIDESLIP STROKE REVIEW

LEVEL 1

- Paddle your boat forward and get a little spin momentum toward the side you are putting your stroke on.
- Put an open-face stern draw in and put pressure on the paddle to pull the boat sideways.

- Control the boat by moving the draw toward the bow or stern as necessary to keep it straight while you are gliding and sliding sideways.

LEVEL 2

- Get up some speed, and put your sideslip stroke in while ferrying.
- Start with your boat on an eddyline and parallel to it. Reach across the eddyline and put your paddle in the current in an open-face normal draw position. Pull your boat into the current sideways and see how far you can ferry on that stroke.

LEVEL 3

- Do the sideslip stroke with a closed-face paddle in the normal draw position. Alternate from right to left and actively pull the blade to your hip. Notice that you can propel the boat forward and pull it sideways at the same time. Pull the paddle straight to the hip; do not do a forward stroke. Since the paddle is closed-face, it will force the boat forward. You can't glide this way, because the paddle will hit the boat and trip you.
- Do the sideslip stroke backward using an open-face bow draw.

43

STROKE	Reverse Sweep Torso Drill
DRILL	30 alternating reverse sweeps: 10 slow, 10 medium, 10 fast
GOALS	To warm up and stretch the torso, biceps, neck and ribs

This drill is purely physiological. You simply paddle backward for thirty strokes using reverse sweeps instead of reverse strokes. This drill does wonders for increasing torso flexibility and stretching out the biceps, thus preventing tendinitis of the elbow, and helping you to separate your body and boat motions.

PADDLE POSITION AND MOVEMENT

See Reverse Sweep. The only difference in this drill is that you are alternating between right and left strokes so that you are paddling backward using reverse sweeps. In order to make this drill have the effect you want, the back arm must be totally straight and you must reach as far to the stern as you can without leaning back. Push the paddle straight away from the stern to maximize the sweeping effect.

BODY POSITION AND MOVEMENT

Keep your body in a neutral or forward position; don't lean back. When you are putting the paddle in the water to start your reverse sweep, rotate your head and body as far as possible, so that you can see your stern and your torso is fully wound up. You will feel your stomach, ribs, neck, biceps (if you are keeping your back arm straight), and pectoral muscles stretching when you start your reverse sweep. Start slowly and gradually build up the amount of effort you put into each stroke so that you don't pull a muscle. Accentuate your body rotation during each stroke so that you get maximum warm-up and stretching effect. This is a critical stretch before playboating, because it warms and stretches the muscles that are at the highest risk of injury.

BOAT POSITION AND MOVEMENT

Keep your boat dead flat during this drill. The tendency is to rock back and forth on each stroke. This shows that either you aren't paying attention or you can't move your body without having the boat move with it. This drill helps you to separate your body and boat motions. This separation is critical for slalom, extreme boating, or playboating, because you often need to rotate, look, lean, or duck, but your boat must stay on course and flat. You also need to control where your boat is heading. You should be able to go in a straight line while your boat is zigzagging.

REVERSE SWEEP TORSO DRILL REVIEW

LEVELS 1, 2, AND 3

- Do ten slow, ten medium, and ten fast reverse sweeps, alternating between left- and right-hand strokes.
- Focus on having your back arm straight and be sure to reach as far back as possible without leaning your body back.

- Be sure your torso and head are wound up so that you can see your stern before each stroke.
- Keep your boat flat during each stroke.
- Keep your boat moving in a straight line, even while zigzagging. If your boat has a squirtable bow, drop your edge to squirt on each stroke.

These are all of the strokes you need to know in flatwater to attain all of your goals in whitewater. This is the entire sport of kayaking, from a stroke and body-position point of view. The mastery of these fundamental drills will bring your paddling to a new level. Any problems you have with any of the strokes or drills are fundamental weaknesses in your paddling that will forever hold you back until you correct them. There are additional drills below for squirting a rodeo or slalom boat and for learning to cartwheel with a rodeo boat. If you don't have a slalom or rodeo boat, you can skip the next two drills and go on to the section on whitewater.

STROKE	Squirting in Flatwater (requires a boat that has a low-volume stern)
DRILL	3 stern squirts in each direction, 360 degrees per squirt
GOALS	To learn the ideal stroke and boat placement for controlled squirting

Squirting a slalom or rodeo boat takes skills in several areas. You need to have a good boat edge control, good body control, and a strong reverse sweep. The boat you are paddling has a lot to do with how easy squirting in flatwater will be. The newer rodeo boats have shorter sterns that make it more difficult to do controlled stern squirts than the earlier squirtable rodeo boats that had longer sterns. Slalom boats in general are very easy to stern squirt (pivot), because the stern is long yet low in volume. This combination gives you more balance, and it's easier to keep the stern underwater because there's a lot of surface area, which prevents it from surfacing quickly. There are numerous ways to learn the stern squirt in flatwater. The method presented here works best for rodeo boats and is the only way to truly learn proper body and boat position without having to fake it.

PADDLE POSITION AND MOVEMENT

There are three strokes during this squirting drill: a forward sweep to get your boat to 90 degrees, a reverse sweep to take it another 180 degrees, and a draw stroke to bring your boat around the final 90 degrees (full 360-degree drill). (Fig. 44–49)

Forward sweep

Start the stern squirt drill by paddling forward as fast as you can, and then letting the boat start to turn in the direction you want to squirt. Assist the spin momentum by doing a forward sweep. Your goal here is to get your boat sliding sideways in the direction your were initially traveling.

Reverse sweep

This is where you get your stern underwater. The technique for the reverse sweep is the same as you learned earlier, except that you need to lean back during the first part of the sweep to assist in sinking the stern. Make the reverse sweep as forceful as you can muster while learning to squirt. You will be able to vary the amount of force once you have the technique down. At the end of the reverse sweep, keep the effort high, because the last part of the reverse sweep has to keep your boat spinning while you take the paddle out of the water.

Draw stroke

You have now rotated 270 degrees. With good balance and edge control, you can make it around the last 90 degrees without another stroke. While learning, however, you should use a draw to ensure that you get around the final 90 degrees. Immediately after taking your paddle out of the water from the reverse sweep, rotate your head and body back in the direction you are spinning in order to wind your torso, then reach your paddle back in the open-face stern-draw position. Now pull your bow around the final 90 degrees. Your paddle goes in the water behind your butt, and you pull it toward your knees. What is actually happening is that you are pulling the boat around until the paddle is by your knees. Try sitting on the floor with your body rotated so that you can grab something stationary behind you. Pull your body until you are facing that object. That's what you are doing during the draw part of the stern squirt.

BODY POSITION AND MOVEMENT
Your body should start in the forward position and stay there for the forward sweep. Keep your body rotated (leading), and lean back for your reverse sweep. Wind your body back up, resetting your head and body, and lean back a little at the beginning of your draw. Finish in a forward position.

BOAT POSITION AND MOVEMENT
Keep your boat flat for the forward sweep so that it can slide. Drop your outside edge into the water at a 30-degree angle for the beginning of the reverse sweep. This is the moment of truth in a squirt. The goal is to slice the stern underwater by angling the boat so that the outside edge catches the oncoming water and cuts into the water, taking the entire stern under with it. This works only if you have sideways speed and you drop your edge into the water at 30 degrees. More angle will cause you to flip over, and less angle won't get the stern underwater. Of course, each boat is different, but 30 degrees works for all squirtable boats. You can keep that edge dropped down only for the first 90 degrees of your reverse sweep. That means you must get the stern underwater at the beginning of your reverse sweep. You must flatten out the boat once you have turned 180 degrees. If you keep the edge dropped after you have finished the reverse sweep, the stern will stall out and pop back up in the direction it came from, and you'll have to brace to avoid falling over. The boat just coasts around the final 180 degrees, with the assistance of the remainder of your reverse sweep and your draw stroke.

FIG. 44 **Get boat spinning . . .**

FIG. 45 **wait until boat spins to 90-degree rotation . . .**

FIG. 46 **lean boat edge to 30-degree angle. Backsweep starts at stern.**

FIG. 47 **Flatten boat edge when boat spins to 180-degree rotation . . .**

FIG. 48 **draw from 270-degree to 360-degree rotation . . .**

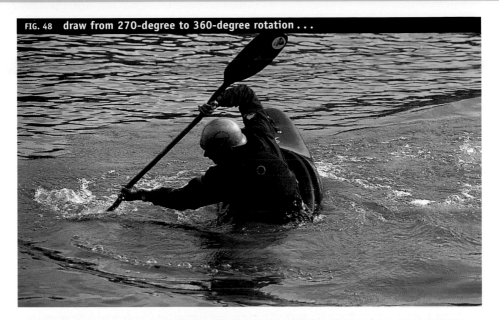

FIG. 49 **continue on your way.**

LEVEL 1

- Get lots of forward speed to start.
- Sweep your boat to 90 degrees to get it sliding sideways.
- Drop your outside edge down in the water at a 30-degree angle, and lock your hips to hold the angle.
- Start your reverse sweep at the stern, leaning back slightly, and push the stern under with force.

- Flatten your boat out when it has spun 180 degrees, and keep it flat.
- Reach back and put an open-face draw in at your stern to bring the boat around the final 90 degrees.
- End in the forward position.

LEVEL 2

- Practice the drill using only the first two strokes, a forward sweep and a reverse sweep, to stern squirt around to 270 degrees. Then coat around the last 90 degrees with your paddle out of the water. You need to have your weight over the boat and control your edges almost perfectly. This works only if your stern is underwater at least a foot at the end of your reverse sweep.
- Practice alternating between the reverse and forward sweeps, keeping the stern underwater the entire time. This is much easier in a slalom boat or a longer squirtable rodeo boat than in the shorter rodeo boats. Drop and edge on every reverse sweep, and hold the boat flat or with only 1 to 5 degrees of edge in the water for the forward sweep. Lead the turn with your head and body; if you get your head and body behind the turn, your stern will come up before you get your next stroke in.

LEVEL 3

- The goal here is to learn to control three factors at one time during a squirt: spinning your boat in a circle; the amount of elevation you have in your bow, or the vertical rotation of the boat; and the rotation of your torso within the kayak. According to Scott Shipley, most people can control only two of the three variables at one time: the spinning of the boat on the horizontal and vertical axes, but not the torso rotation. Only when you can comfortably control all three can you do what you want with your boat during a squirt, because you can have your body in position for your next direction change at any time. You know you have it down when your boat makes a smooth rotation while you are resting your shoulders, and you can do as many repetitions as you want without falling over.

- Squirt on a back sweep.
- Reset your shoulders to lead the turn, while letting the boat come around another 90 degrees, with the paddle out of the water.
- Forward sweep another 90 degrees, keeping your weight forward and shoulders leading the turn.
- Repeat.

STROKE	Initiation Stroke (cartwheel drill for playboating)
DRILL	10 bobs on each side, with no loss of balance or motion
GOALS	To learn how to initiate your bow or stern on demand for cartwheeling

This drill is easiest with a boat that is 9 feet or shorter and has balanced volume from bow to stern. The initiation stroke drill simply involves putting your boat on edge, 45 degrees, and rocking it back and forth so that the bow and stern bob up and down in the water. The purpose of the drill is to learn how to push your bow underwater to get a cartwheel going, and to pull the stern underwater to get a cartwheel going off the stern. If you can't get the ends of your boat underwater on demand, you won't be able to cartwheel. This drill teaches you to balance in the cartwheel position and to have good, strong initiation strokes. Every boat bobs at a different rate, so you have to be with your boat's rate and not fight its natural movement.

PADDLE POSITION AND MOVEMENT

With your paddle in the forward sweep position, sweep your bow into the air. (Since your boat is on edge, the bow will go up instead of off to the side.) Immediately push your top hand in front of you so that you are in a reverse sweep position, and push the bow back down with a reverse sweep. (Fig. 50–55) Repeat over and over: push-pull, push-pull with your paddle. The key is to be quick. Beginners tend to push and pull fruitlessly, because the boat wants to bob up and down at a rate faster than they are stroking. Think of it this way: You sweep your stern under, and the air in the stern makes it pop back out of the water. Your goal is to assist that process by doing a back sweep that helps lift the stern out and push the bow in. When the bow goes in, you want to assist it back up to the surface and the stern back under. In general, the pace is about two bobs per second. If you are going slower than that, your boat will not respond as you would like. Don't expect this drill to come easily. It requires a lot of practice.

BODY POSITION AND MOVEMENT

Keep your body weight over your boat and start in the neutral position. In this drill your body is a kind of axis around which your boat will rotate. The bow and stern of your boat will be bobbing in and out of the water as you throw the ends with your torso while using the paddle strokes described above. Throwing your weight forward at the bow initiation and backward at the stern initiation helps drive the edges of your boat deeper into the water, allowing you to get a more vertical position.

BOAT POSITION AND MOVEMENT

Keep the boat at a 45-degree angle lean. Think of this drill as using your boat as a rocking horse. You will be leaning the boat over at a 45-degree angle and making it rock up and down so the bow and stern go in and out of the water.

FIG. 50 Lift bow up . . .

FIG. 51 reverse the power to come back down . . .

FIG. 52 push the bow under . . .

FIG. 53   slam the stern down using your momentum . . .

FIG. 54   bow under again . . .

FIG. 55   weight stays over the boat for balance.

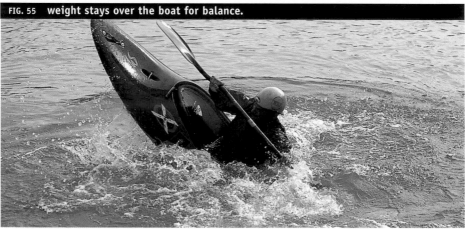

Applying the Strokes and Concepts to Whitewater

You now know everything you need to know about kayaking strokes in flatwater. This is exciting because it means you know all of the strokes for whitewater as well. You now need to learn the applications to whitewater and make them habit. The flatwater drills are the only way to learn the strokes and to improve them each time you paddle. Applying the strokes to whitewater is all about control, efficiency, consistency, simplicity, and speed. Just as in flatwater, where learning to use the draw properly reduced the number of strokes necessary, learning proper whitewater applications can reduce the number of strokes you need while allowing you to go faster and have more control. The sport has progressed so far in the past few years in terms of equipment, strokes, and skills that few boaters, including instructors, possess the proper whitewater skills.

FOUR WHITEWATER CONCEPTS

Whitewater has energy that can be harnessed by your boat and paddle. The faster the water, the more energy you can harness. In kayaking there are two sources of energy to direct and propel your boat: you must use your own energy, or use the river's energy. The best kayakers use a combination of both.

Current itself isn't a source of energy that you can use to propel your boat. For instance, if you are floating down a fast-moving flat river, then relative to the water, you are stationary. There are four concepts that affect your kayak during these critical moments when you have potential energy.

1. **Speed:** the velocity of your kayak either forward or backward relative to the water you are sitting in. For example, having speed out of an eddy means you paddled hard while in the eddy and are crossing the eddyline with speed.

2. **Angle:** the angle of your boat relative to an eddyline, the current in a wave, the backwash of a hole, or the current in a hole.

3. **Spin Momentum:** the direction in which your kayak is spinning when it is moving forward or backward.

4. **Arc:** the path your body and boat take, from a bird's-eye view. All moves in whitewater are done in an arc, never in a straight line.

Most of the boaters that possess the skills are focused on slalom racing and not bringing the level of skills of kayakers everywhere up to date.

Does that mean that slalom racers know their strokes? No, only a few racers in the U.S. have any knowledge of these techniques. Slalom racing is a test of control, speed, and efficiency and is constantly breeding new techniques for achieving these goals. Scott Shipley was the most helpful in developing the latest, up-to-date concepts and techniques—the same concepts and techniques that we are learning here.

Let's get to it!

Eddy Turns

Peeling out and eddying out are the most important and basic skills in whitewater. Every move is based on these techniques: whether peeling out onto a wave for a rodeo, catching a critical eddy in the middle of a Class V rapid, or just peeling out to head downriver. You will learn to peel out and eddy out using the same technique every time. Remember, your goals are maximum control, speed, and efficiency.

PEEL OUT THEORY
Speed: In general, crossing the eddyline with some speed is advisable. Because the eddyline is where two opposing currents meet, it is one of the most awkward places on the river. The more speed you have when you cross an eddyline, the less time you will spend there, and the less turning effect the current will have on your boat.

Angle: You should always peel out at an angle that doesn't require a correction stroke after you get into the current. In general, you can let the bow turn downstream after you peel out, but it's more difficult to bring the bow back upstream after it washes down.

Spin Momentum: You want spin momentum to take you downstream on a peel-out, although there are times that spin momentum that goes upstream is preferable, such as when doing attainments.

Arc: A smooth, consistent arc is the most controllable, fastest, and most efficient way to travel in your kayak.

This means keeping a constant radius in your turn.

Now that we know how we want our boat to be moving for the peel-out, let's choose the appropriate strokes.

PEEL-OUT STROKES
While in the eddy, use forward strokes to gain speed. As your boat begins to cross the eddyline, reach across the eddyline with your downstream paddle blade, and do a powerful forward stroke to pull your butt entirely across the eddyline. Convert your forward stroke into a closed-face stern draw without taking the paddle out of the water. The last stroke as you peel out is always the same: a forward stroke that starts before and finishes after your butt crosses the eddyline. The paddle stays in the water and you cock your wrist forward and rotate your head and body toward the paddle to do a stern draw. (Fig. 56–60) Why do we need these exact strokes? The forward stroke serves to boost and maintain forward speed as the boat crosses the eddyline. The stroke is done on the downstream side of the boat both to counteract the force of the water on the upstream side, and to control the amount of spin momentum you have. The closed-face stern draw then controls the arc and maintains the appropriate spin momentum and angle. In using the closed-face stern draw, we are using our paddle to propel and control our kayak in much the same way that sails and keels propel and control sailboats.

FIG. 56 Get speed in eddy . . .

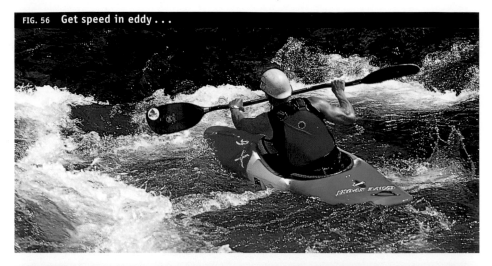

FIG. 57 reach across eddyline for final forward stroke . . .

FIG. 58 pull butt across eddyline with forward stroke . . .

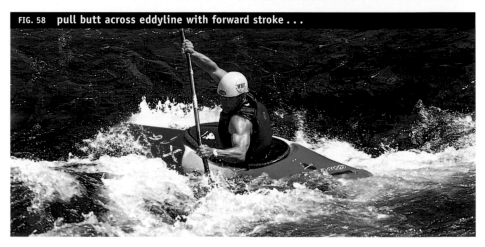

FIG. 59   convert into stern draw . . .

FIG. 60   keep stern draw closed-face.

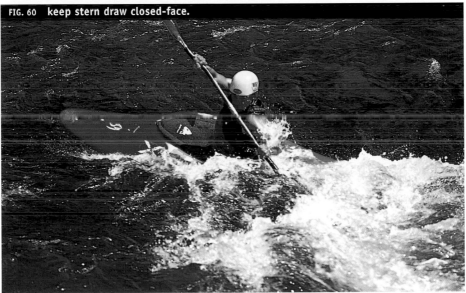

Sails capture the energy from the wind (or water, in this case) and convert the energy into forward speed for the boat, no matter what direction it is moving, except directly into the current or wind. Sails are so effective that they can cause a boat to go faster than the wind or current propelling it. You need three things in order to use your paddle as a sail.

1. Current differentials (such as at eddylines or holes) or wave energy.
2. A keel to keep your kayak from sliding: a draw stroke at or behind the center of gravity, your butt. Spin momentum allows the keel to work behind the center of gravity without the boat's sliding.
3. Proper blade angles to capture the current and convert it to forward or backward speed, equivalent to sheeting in or sheeting out.

What do you do after you have crossed the eddyline and you have a stern draw in the water? Remember your three rules for every turn (from the discussion of spin momentum): lead every turn with your head and body, control every turn on the inside, and use a draw to control every turn.

EDDY OUT THEORY

The same techniques described for peeling out are used for eddying out.

You need to understand your objectives when catching eddies. Sure, you can mush across an eddyline, slide backward for a few feet, take four or five strokes back upstream to get where you want to be in the eddy, and hang out until you are ready to leave. That is far below your potential, however, and it will ultimately lead to missing important eddies, getting tired early, and having lots of problems on big water with boily eddylines, among other things. In general, the objective is to get across the eddyline and lock into the eddy at its top or at a chosen spot, if you plant to stop in the eddy. Another option is to S-turn through an eddy in the middle of the river. Let's look at catching eddies first.

EDDY OUT TECHNIQUES

The following general technique works in most situations to lock into an eddy:

1. Set up your eddy turn in advance by angling your boat toward the eddy long before getting there.
2. Get up some crosscurrent speed by taking a few strokes toward the eddyline before you reach it. (Fig. 61) This requires you to start in the middle of the river.
3. Reach across the eddyline and pull yourself across it with a forward stroke on the upstream side (Fig. 62), converting it into a stern draw, exactly as described for peeling out. (Fig. 63)
4. Allow the boat to turn until you are facing the shore. Hold the boat straight to the shore until you are as deep in the eddy as you want to go (Fig. 64), then feather your blade forward, allowing the boat to turn upstream. You can pull on the blade, after you feather it forward, to take you as far up the eddy as you need.

FIG. 61 **Crosscurrent momentum . . .**

FIG. 62 **forward stroke across eddyline . . .**

FIG. 63 **convert to stern draw . . .**

FIG. 64 **glide deep into eddy.**

STROKE	**Eddy Turn. Forward stroke to pull yourself across the eddyline, followed by a closed-face stern draw. You should feather your paddle from the forward stroke into the draw**
DRILL	**Peel out of an eddy and carve a turn until you are facing downstream. After establishing yourself, turn your boat back toward the eddy. Eddy out using the same technique used to peel out, then glide on the stern draw to get as deep into the eddy as you can get. Practice entering the eddy at different angles**
GOALS	**A smooth, wide arc on the exit (upstream to crosscurrent to downstream momentum) and on the reentry (downstream to crosscurrent to upstream momentum). Accelerate on your draw using the river's energy**

The following are some common misconceptions about eddy turns.

Misconception: You should paddle up to an eddy to do a sweep to turn the boat into the eddy.

Explanation: It is risky and often unsuccessful to wait until you are right at the eddy to turn your boat into the eddy. You must turn the boat at the right time and get the proper angle, all while trying to cross the eddyline.

If you set your angle upstream of the eddy, you can just float until you are in the right position and then take two or three strokes to get to the eddyline. You don't have time to turn; you can do it well in advance and then focus on hitting the eddyline at the precise spot you have chosen.

Misconception: You should bow draw into the eddy.

Explanation: Bow draws are unnecessary. Pick up the angle and speed across the eddyline that allow you to draw at the hip and lock into the eddy. If you don't keep your draw at the hip when you cross the eddy, you will slide downstream. You have both downstream and crosscurrent momentum when entering an eddy, and you need to convert that momentum into upstream momentum. That requires a proper draw.

There are a lot of situations that make for less-than-ideal eddy turns. Make sure you practice using techniques that are as close to ideal as possible. When approaching a very small, narrow eddy with no room to glide deep into it, come in pointed straight to shore, with lots of crosscurrent speed but little downstream speed. Pull yourself across the eddyline into the normal draw position, pull hard toward the boat on the draw for an instant to lock in, and immediately feather the blade to your knees and do a C-stroke to bring you to the top of the eddy. You only need an eddy large enough to get your butt across the eddyline before the bow hits the shore for this to work. If it's smaller than that, you'll have to ferry in.

EDDY TURN DRILL

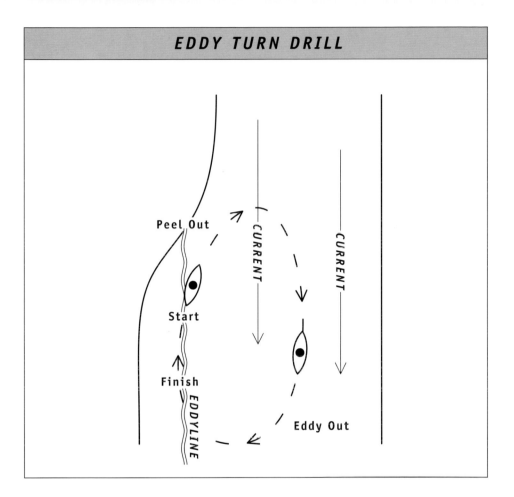

STROKE	Ferrying. Forward stroke to pull yourself across the eddyline, followed by a closed-face stern draw. You should feather your paddle from the forward stroke into the draw
DRILL	Practice ferrying out as far as possible with one stroke, using different boat and blade angles to learn the effect of each and to be able to intuitively pick the right speed, angle, arc, spin momentum, and draw position to get where you want to go
GOALS	To ferry under control, and to use the current to accelerate your boat across the river to the destination of your choice with one stroke

Ferrying is moving across the river using the river's energy to drive your kayak to the desired destination. There is no difference between an eddy turn and a ferry in terms of general theory and technique. A ferry requires the same speed, angle, and spin momentum necessary for a good peel-out; therefore, the same strokes should be used. The fundamental difference between an eddy turn and a ferry is the difference in the path of the arc: rather than gradually converting upstream momentum into downstream momentum as you would for a peel-out, you convert the upstream momentum to crosscurrent momentum.

When you exit an eddy, on fairly stable water with no huge boils, you should be able to ferry to any desired destination on one draw stroke. This is true for most rivers that are less than 5,000 cubic feet per second and 75 feet wide. Larger rivers will require that you start paddling again with forward strokes to get to the other side. Crossing on one stroke may seem impossible if you haven't tried it or seen anyone paddle this way but it really works! You will eliminate four to six strokes from each peel-out or ferry, have much greater control, and have much more speed to your destination.

Note: This section features moves that, like peeling out, involve *multiple* strokes.

FERRYING DRILL

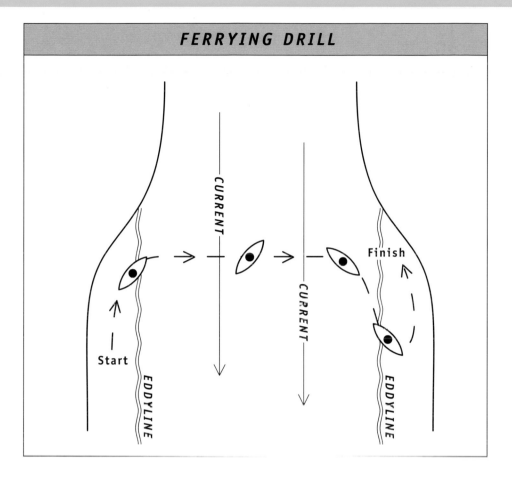

Get up speed in the eddy, using forward strokes, and approach the eddyline at a 45-degree angle. Reach across the eddyline and pull your butt across it with a forward stroke, converting the forward stroke into a closed-face stern draw. Apply pressure to the stroke by holding the stern draw close to the boat. The current will try to drag your paddle away from your boat. Hold the paddle in position so that the water will pull your paddle, boat, and body across the river and accelerate you, similar in effect to the wind in a sail. The size of the arc you take is determined by the position of your paddle. If it is really far back to the stern and you are holding a lot of pressure on it, you will not turn downstream at all but will ferry. If you have it close to the center of the boat (your butt), you will turn quickly downstream and won't be able to ride the draw as long. It's your job to keep the draw at your stern long enough to get as far as you want across the river, then feather the paddle forward to let the bow turn downstream. Remember that you want a smooth, steady arc. If you turn quickly downstream after leaving the eddy, you can forget gliding, efficiency, and speed. If you make a quick 180-degree turn after the ferry, you won't be using the current at all. Take a wide arc out of the eddy by holding the stern draw until you are far enough out into the current for your next destination. Your draw can move forward or backward to keep the boat on the path you want. The instant you take the draw out of the water, you are no longer in control or using the river's energy, so don't take it out until you have completely turned downstream or you want to turn the other way.

When ferrying onto waves, use the same technique, staying on the stern draw until you have established yourself on the wave.

FERRYING INTO AN EDDY

Often you'll have to ferry into an eddy, such as when you are playboating or catching an eddy that you saw too late. When ferrying into an eddy, the eddyline will tend to reject your boat and prevent you from getting into the eddy. You need to get your entire boat past the eddyline. The forward stroke across the eddyline is the same for a normal eddy turn. Keep the bow pointed toward the shore by pulling (and sweeping) on the upstream side only, until you are completely in the eddy. Try to avoid being turned parallel to the eddyline.

Whitewater S-turns

An S-turn in whitewater is done across eddies that are in the middle of the river so that there is current on both sides of the eddy. It is simply going in one side of the eddy and coming out the other. The S-turn is the fastest, most efficient way to get from one side of the river to another. Any time you are running a rapid and there are eddies in the middle of the river, you have opportunities to use those eddies to get where you want to go without many strokes.

The ideal S-turn starts the same as a regular eddy turn. (Fig. 65) You begin with downstream angle and pull yourself across the eddyline with a forward stroke that turns into a stern draw. (Fig. 67) Keep the draw in the water and your boat pointed straight across the eddy toward the far shore until you reach the other side of the eddy. Convert your draw into a forward stroke and pull. (Fig. 68) Then, reach across the eddyline with your other blade, and use the standard peel-out technique, consisting of a forward stroke that turns into a stern draw in the current as you head back downstream. (Fig. 69–70) You can glide across most eddies on one stroke. The S-turn in whitewater is very much like the S-turn stroke drill in flatwater. It is actually much easier to keep the boat moving because of the energy you pick up when you cross the eddyline.

FIG. 65 **Same entry as eddy turn . . .**

FIG. 66 don't allow bow to turn upstream on entry . . .

FIG. 67 glide across eddy on closed-face stern draw . . .

FIG. 68 convert draw to forward stroke . . .

FIG. 69   pull boat out of eddy with forward stroke . . .

FIG. 70   convert to draw.

WHITEWATER S-TURN REVIEW

LEVEL 1

- Enter the eddy as you would for a normal eddy turn.
- Keep your bow pointed at the far shore until you hit the next eddyline.
- When you cross the eddyline on the way out, switch to a forward stroke that turns into a stern draw, as you would for a normal peel-out.

- Put your boat slightly on the inside edge on the way in and then again on the way out. Extreme leans are not necessary or beneficial.

LEVEL 2

- Pick an arc that gives you the peel-out angle you want when you get to the other side of the eddy. For example, if you wanted to cross the eddy and then ferry to the other side of the river, you would allow the bow to turn up more in the eddy so that you would exit the eddy with a good ferry angle.

- Practice gliding across the eddy with a closed-face stern draw. You can keep up your speed that way.
- Practice using the backwash of pour-overs or flat holes as the eddy to S-turn.

LEVEL 3

- Practice using all kinds of holes to S-turn. The trick is to lean into the turn (upstream) on the entry. You need to get your boat on top of the backwash so that you don't catch your upstream edge. If you lean downstream when you hit the hole, you'll stop dead. You should paddle with speed to the corner of the hole and jump on top from a 45-degree angle. As soon as your boat hits the foampile, you begin leaning upstream and pull yourself on top of the hole, using a forward stroke that feathers into a draw on the upstream side of your boat.

Holes

Holes are the single most common source of fear on a river run by beginners, intermediates, and even experts. This fear is usually fear of the unknown: Will that hole stop me? If I get surfed, will I be able to get out? Can I roll in a hole? Most kayakers have too little experience with holes to know what to expect, so the goal becomes avoiding them. Avoiding holes becomes a habit, and then the kayaker has a problem. There are only so many features in a river that you can use: the current, waves, rocks, eddies, and holes. If you eliminate holes, you are operating with only 80 percent of the possible features.

Planing hull (flat-bottom) boats are more stable in holes than are displacement hull (curved-bottom) boats. Planing hull boats are generally wider and offer more stability, which is accentuated when they are planing, due to the water rushing under them when you are sitting sideways in a hole. They also have less resistance to the oncoming water when sideways, so they don't get pushed into the foampile as far and thus provide a more stable and smoother ride.

There are several things you need to know to be able to use holes to maneuver or play. First, you need to understand the hole before you enter it. Once you've entered a hole, you need to know how to stay upright, how to roll, and how to get out.

FIG. 71 **Pulling through a hole.**

Understanding the hole before your enter it

There are three kinds of holes: wave-holes, true holes, and pourover holes.

A *wave-hole* occurs when the oncoming water goes down into a trough and, upon rising, falls back onto itself thus creating a foampile on top of the wave. This kind of hole is easiest to surf because the oncoming water approaches smoothly and at a low angle. Also, it is frequently more difficult to stay in a wave-hole than it is to get out. This type of hole is the best bet for learning hole-surfing technique. A *true hole* occurs where the oncoming water meets the foampile at the trough of the hole, yet the oncoming water approaches at an angle of 60 degrees or less. A *pourover* occurs where the water drops almost vertically off a ledge or over a rock to form a hole that has significant back-wash and very little water flowing downstream through it. It is more difficult to brace and maneuver in a pourover, because you have to lean so far downstream to avoid catching your upstream edge.

STAYING UPRIGHT

A hole tends to want to hold you sideways in it. It also wants to grab your upstream edge and power-flip you upstream. In order to stay upright and be balanced, you need to lean your boat downstream so the hull is sitting flat on the oncoming water. For example, if the water coming into the hole is dropping at an angle of 30 degrees, then you need to lean your boat 30 degrees downstream so that the water planes off of the hull. If you lean too much downstream, you'll have to brace hard to stay upright.

BRACING

Bracing in a hole is easy. The water going under your boat offers plenty of support for your brace. Either a high or low brace will keep your boat upright. For a high brace, keep the paddle's power face down, elbows under the paddle, and the paddle perpendicular to the boat. For a low brace, keep the paddle's back face against the water, elbows over the paddle, and the paddle perpendicular to the boat. Which brace to use depends on whether you want to move your boat forward or backward. To move forward, use a high brace. To move backward, use a low brace. The brace should be in front of your body, and the paddle shaft should be perpendicular to your boat. It doesn't require much force on the paddle to stay upright if you are keeping your weight over the boat and keeping the boat angle the same as the water coming down into the hole.

ROLLING IN A HOLE

Rolling is easier in a hole than anywhere else, including flatwater. In a hole, the water tries to roll you back up; you only need to help it. If you feel yourself being flipped in a hole, the first thing to do is relax. Don't fight it. There's nothing you can do once you begin flipping upstream in a hole. If you try to brace as you're going over, you'll likely hit bottom with your paddle and either break it or hurt your shoulder. By relaxing, you are keeping your paddle still and perpendicular to your boat, and keeping your head forward and face down. Most of the time, flipping upstream in a hole is very safe, even if the hole is shallow. This is because the oncoming water pushes you downstream into the foampile, and your boat pops up a bit when your body enters the water, keeping you in deeper water and your body shallow. Holes are very forgiving that way, and we can be grateful for that!

Once you've flipped over, the oncoming water will pull your body downstream and then try to lift up on the downstream side. This is the side you should roll up on. If you relax and keep your paddle on your sprayskirt and perpendicular to the boat, you only have to brace with the paddle, and do a hip snap to roll up. No fancy setup technique is required. You'll know you are trying to roll up on the wrong side if you can't get your paddle to go where you want it. You need to practice your off-side hip snaps and braces, because you have 50 percent chance of being on your off side. Even if you can't roll on both sides in flatwater, you'll be able to roll on both sides in a hole.

After you've rolled up, resume the bracing position. If you forget to keep leaning your boat downstream after hip-snapping up, you'll keep rolling over upstream. This unpleasant, but fun-to-watch action is known as windowshading.

GETTING OUT OF A HOLE

In general, there are three places to exit a hole: at the end of the hole on river right, on river left, or out through the foampile in the middle of it. Though there are all kinds of experiences you can have in a hole as you surf or try to exit it, the one constant is that you have to eventually get out of it or you'll have to swim. Swimming is an option we won't discuss here. To get out of a hole is to understand how to maneuver in a hole. Depending on the type of hole, you may be able to pull out forward, back out, ender out, or blast out of the hole. Whether you go forward or backward out of a hole, when you reach the edge, your boat will begin to turn downstream, and the oncoming water will try to catch your upstream edge and flip you upstream. This will tip you over, but it will also help you get out of the hole. Remember that tipping over is OK, even a good thing.

Pulling out

If you want to pull yourself forward out of the hole, start with a high brace. Cock your right wrist down about 45 degrees, which will give you 50 percent bracing and 50 percent forward stroke with your paddle. Now, if you push your paddle in the water, the water rushing downstream will try to pull you forward and will support your brace. If you need more power to get out the side of the hole, you can raise your left arm to get the paddle more vertical, giving you more of a forward stroke to pull forward. Be careful, however, not to raise your hand too high above your shoulder, as you risk shoulder injury. You need enough momentum to get out of the hole. The deeper the hole, the more momentum and power you'll need to get out of it. If you try to pull forward to get out and you stall out and can't pull yourself all the way out, don't worry. You just need to relax, let the hole bring you back into the trough, and start again, getting more momentum from the beginning to break out. If this doesn't work, then try backing out.

Backing out

Backing out is similar to pulling out, except that you push backward with a low brace. Starting in the low brace position, cock your right wrist back 45 degrees, which will give you 50 percent bracing and 50 percent backstroke. Push the paddle into the water, and the oncoming water will give you support for bracing and allow you to push yourself backward. Try to create as much momentum as you can from the start to break out of the hole. You can alternate backing up and then pulling forward to get up as much speed as possible.

Endering out

It is also possible to have the downstream-flowing water push you out through the hole by launching over the foampile. This can be easy or difficult, depending on the hole. In order to ender out of a hole, you must be able to move to the side of the hole by high or low bracing and pulling yourself out to the side. Often holes let you to the side easily but don't let you out the very end, because there's a hill to climb that slows your momentum. In this case, your boat will start to exit the hole and turn downstream, but you will get pulled back in, and your bow or stern will catch the oncoming water and be pushed underwater, catapulting your boat downstream. Most often, the ender is not vertical but is more of an upstream flip that gets your boat about 45 degrees in the air. Here, you'll usually vault over the foampile and out of the hole.

Blasting out

Blasting out of a hole is just surfing the hole, with the foampile pushing on your back and the hull planing off the oncoming water. From this position, the oncoming water tries to surf you to one side or another with lots of speed. This allows you to use the energy in the foampile and oncoming water, thus front-surfing right out of a hole without having to climb out. The technique is to do a powerful front sweep while you are side-surfing to force your stern under the foampile. Lean back and continue your sweep into a stern draw to help get the stern under and the bow on top of the approaching water. Keep the stern draw in the water, and surf out the side. You need to practice blasting to learn to control it well. Wave-holes are the best kind of holes for learning to blast, and pourovers are the most difficult. If you want to use blasting as a technique in holes, you need to have a shorter playboat.

Going out the bottom

To go out the bottom of a hole, you can let yourself flip upstream and hope you wash out. This works only for holes that have a nonretentive foampile. The size of the hole isn't the determining factor, only the amount of water that goes through it versus the amount of water coming back upstream. If you don't wash out, you'll have to put your downstream paddle blade in the water and use a hip snap to roll back up.

HOLES REVIEW

STAYING UPRIGHT IN A HOLE

- Keep your weight centered over the boat.
- Keep your hull flat on the oncoming water (lean your boat downstream to keep the upstream edge from catching).

- Keep your paddle in the water in either a high or low brace position.

MANEUVERING IN A HOLE

- Use a high brace with a closed face to pull yourself forward. Pull against the water, going under the foampile.

- Use a low brace and cock your wrist up and back so you can push yourself backward in the hole.

ROLLING IN A HOLE

- Relax and let yourself go when you feel yourself catching an edge and going over.
- Keep your paddle on your sprayskirt and perpendicular to the boat. This sets you up for the roll.

- Keep your body forward and head down when flipping over.
- Brace yourself back up on the downstream side with a high brace and a controlled hip snap.

Wave Surfing

This is not a playboating book, so the goal in this section is to teach you how to control yourself on waves so you can use them in your river running. You need to practice ferrying, using the techniques described above, and be comfortable with turning a forward stroke into a stern draw before practicing wave techniques. No matter what level you currently paddle at, you should use the peel-out technique to cross the eddy-line onto a wave.

There are three elements to surfing a wave: getting there, being there, and going somewhere else. Getting on a wave is best done from an eddy that allows you to peel out onto the wave from directly beside it. Ideally, your technique will put you on the wave the first time, every time, and in control. (Fig. 72–76) To do this, you want to eliminate as many variables as possible before you cross the eddyline, leaving only the minimum amount of maneuvering for once you're on the actual wave.

Variables you must control

1. How far up or down the wave your boat is when you catch it.
   - Your butt should be just in front of the peak of the wave as you enter the wave from the side. If it is way in front of the peak, in the trough, you'll have difficulty keeping your bow up and controlling the bow once you are on it. If you're behind the peak, you'll miss the wave entirely.
   - You eliminate this variable by peeling out of the eddy when your butt is just in front of the peak. You can always maintain control in the flatwater of an eddy. So before you start, pick the path out of the eddy that puts you where you need to be.

2. Whether your momentum is going up- or downstream.
   - Ideally, you get on the wave from the side with no up- or downstream momentum. This way, you can get on the wave just in front of the peak and stay there.
   - You control your speed while entering the wave by exiting the eddy in the right spot with the right speed. You wouldn't sprint across the eddyline onto a wave that is easy to get to from the side, because you'd ride right down the face of the wave into the trough instantly. You need to cross the eddyline with the right speed. It would be similar to jumping onto a moving treadmill. If you simply sprang up onto it, you'd be dragged right into the bars at the end. You would have to jump on it from the side while running the same speed as the treadmill was going.

- Once you have the necessary forward speed, you can reach across the eddyline and pull yourself sideways onto the face of the wave.
3. How much angle you have to the wave.
    - You'll control your exit angle out of the eddy with your stern draw. If you're at an angle at which you could ferry across the river, then you're also at an angle that will work for surfing.
4. Which way your spin momentum is going.
    - When you get onto a wave, you'll surf right across to the other side and off it unless you turn back. With the stern draw in the water, you can convert your spin momentum back into the eddy as soon as you cross the eddyline.

5. What strokes you take.
    - Use the peel-out technique to get yourself established on the wave. After you're surfing, you can use a rudder to control the surf. If you try to use the rudder too soon, before crossing the eddyline, it won't always work. It's critical to have the option of a power stroke as you enter the wave, which you have with the forward stroke that turns into a stern draw. Once you begin to use the rudder, you're actually forcing the boat downstream. If you start losing the bow, you'll have to rudder harder and you'll pull yourself right off the wave.

Now you are there and ready to stay there.

Have fun!

FIG. 72 Lining up for a sideslip stroke onto a wave . . .

FIG. 73   reaching opened-face stern draw into current . . .

FIG. 74   pulling boat across eddyline . . .

FIG. 75 sliding onto the face of the wave . . .

FIG. 76 your surf is established.